D0542675

About t

Ceri Worman is a new and exciting talent in children's books. She has been a teacher, a librarian and a teacher of English in Uruguay. After studying for an MA in creative writing, Ceri came up with Jamie B, a funny, energetic character who leads an exciting secret life. Ceri says, 'As a child, I lived a secret life too, through the books I read. Now I do it by writing them!'

In her real life Ceri is a children's librarian who lives in Barnsley with her teenage son. This is her third book about...The Secret Life of Jamie B.

Reviews for *The Secret Life of Jamie B, Superspy*

'Entertaining, pacy, with wide appeal. One to recommend.' *Books for Keeps*

'Hard to put down. I really enjoyed the book.'
Blair Watson in *Teen Titles*

'A good, fast-moving thriller...with plenty of humour.' *School Librarian*

To Marcus and his game-playing mates.

Ceri wishes to thank Fiona Bruce and the following pupils from Westborough High School, Dewsbury: Shozab Abbas, Mofia Akbar, Ismail Valli, Korey Hubbard, Ben Broderik, Jordan Pugh, Ahmad Ramzan, Oliver Brooke, Ismaeel Patel and Nathan Frazer. They read the manuscript and fed her foodfight tips!

ORCHARD BOOKS
96 Leonard Street, London EC2A 4XD
Hachette Children's Books Australia
Level 17/207 Kent Street, Sydney NSW 2000
First published in Great Britain in 2005
ISBN 1 84362 946 1
A paperback original
Text © Ceri Worman 2005
The right of Ceri Worman to be identified as the author of this work has been asserted by her in accordance with the Copyright, Designs and Patents Act, 1988
A CIP catalogue record for this book is available from the British Library.
Printed in Great Britain
1 3 5 7 9 10 8 6 4 2

THE SECRET LIFE OF JAMIE B

HERO.COM

Ceri Worman

ORCHARD BOOKS

Camden Libraries	
42064500	
DirectBooks	25/05/2006
	£4.99

Contents

Contents

LEVEL 1

Ring of Fire

Welcome to the world of cyberJ@hero.com!
Please enter your password...

Yes, Jamie B (one-time superspy, one-time rapstar), has *evolved*. Now I'm a hero and not just your everyday hero. I'm a computer game hero – a hero.com.

So, meet cyberJ – the ultimate hero in the Game. And I'm ready to move on up to a totally different level.

Cool and mean, cyberJ's mind is his ultimate weapon. He uses stealth and strategy to save the world, kick enemy butt and win the love of a beautiful 3D cyberbabe.

It's Monday morning and my fingers itch to play a computer game right now and practise my skills, but there's a glitch in the system. School.

There must be more to life than this! I stare into the mirror and look for an **Escape** key when …EEeeyaagh! Who's that staring back at me?

Is it some kind of mutant cyberJ-clone? I've got a shadow on my top lip and strange red circles on my chin. Any minute now they're going to explode…

Level 1:	**Ring of Fire**
Location:	**Planet Earth**
Task:	**The Ring of Fire chain of volcanoes is about to explode and destroy the world. Only a cyberhero can stop it.**

10–9

Scroll down Weapons Menu

Select> *Red-Hot-Spot-Blaster*

8–7

Scroll down Skills Menu

Select> *Teleport*

6–5

Faster than a brain-wave, cyberJ blurs across the world, his long black

coat streaming out behind him.

4–3

CyberJ hovers above the glowing craters of the Ring of Fire, his stylish shades shielding his eyes from the intense heat.

2–1...

Angry bubbles of steam hit the air – any minute now they are going to blow. CyberJ points the *Red-Hot-Spot-Blaster* down into the heart of the volcano.

B o o m!

Boiling lava explodes into the air. Showering ash turns day into night. Is it Game Over for cyberJ?

Suddenly the volcanoes freeze mid-spurt—

YOU WIN, CYBERJ!

GO TO THE NEXT LEVEL...

'Jamie, why are you crashing and bashing about in the bathroom? Hurry up and get ready for school!'

'Yeah, two minutes,' I yell, picking up the deodorant, shampoo and toothpaste I somehow knocked over in my spot-shock alert.

The voice-over is cyberM. She's my Creator. It's hard to believe she spawned me – cyberJ, the Special One – but I've seen the photo albums.

Having a Creator on the scene can be very annoying – they try to control every move you make – but she does have her uses, too. Like now when my energy levels need a boost. So I go downstairs to refuel after **Bathroom Battle 1: Ring of Fire.**

CyberM waves her car keys at me while I slurp my cereal standing at the kitchen sink and says, 'I thought I'd take you to school today, Jamie.'

Why is she breaking the rules of the Game? CyberM *never* drives me to school. Her instructions clearly state that I must always walk, otherwise we'll clog up the world with petrol fumes and destroy the universe as we know it.

We get in the car and cyberM pulls out onto the road. 'Jamie, I wanted us to have some time for a mature, grown-up conversation,' she says.

'Sure, how can I help?' I reply in a mature and grown-up voice. 'Oh yeah…I need a bottle of *Red-Hot-Spot-Blaster*. It says on TV that it stops spots in seconds. It's an emergency!' I add, catching sight of myself in the wing mirror.

'Sorry, you'll have to wait till tomorrow. I'm busy after work today. That's what I wanted to talk about—'

'And can you pick up a razor too? You said I was grown-up, and I think it's time to start shaving.'

'Not *that* grown-up, Jamie. You're not even a teenager till next month. Now, let's see how mature you can be about this. We've got a visitor coming for tea tonight. It's a man. A friend. A special friend...'

An enemy invader in my cyberspace? A hero.com shows no emotion. 'Who is it? Anyone I know?' I ask, casually.

'Yes...remember I did that business studies evening class at your school? That's how I met Mr Tempus – your Maths teacher. Now count to ten, Jamie.'

1–2

I can feel my fists clench, my shoulders tense, my face get hot.

3–4

'And there's one other thing you should know...'

5–6

I nod. I can't speak. CyberM going out with a teacher? She has broken the **Sacred Cybercode** and gone over to the dark side. I remain cool and silent. I will betray no feeling.

7–8

'Mr Tempus will have his daughter with him. She's in your year at school, I think.'

9–10

Noooo! Not Anna! Not her! She's totally weird – and as annoying as a spot on your—

BOOM!

'Jamie, calm down! Control yourself! Jamie, I'm going to stop the car, right now! You can walk the rest of the way to school. I think you need to let off steam!'

Suddenly I find myself on the pavement a few streets away from Grimly High School. I remember there was a lot of noise and a car door slammed shut.

Calm down, cyberM said, but I'm feeling totally wired. My head's buzzing and my hands are shaking.

Game over. I blew it.

LEVEL 2

Tempus the Evil Time Warrior

So I'm walking down Grimly High Street feeling totally out of it when I notice something strange. Where is everyone? The wind is blowing, it's starting to rain and I feel like I'm the last human left in the world.

Usually there are lots of other kids going to school at this time...then I look at my watch and see that I'm late. Very late.

How did that happen? Where did the time go? I've just lost fifteen minutes on my life-meter. The Game must be faulty. How do you get an upgrade?

My head is full of questions but there's one thing for sure – if I'm late again this month, I get a detention.

Time to launch a stealth mission.

Looking moody and mysterious in my long, black school coat, heavy boots and shades I turn the corner of Grimly Lane and scan the school gates. There, standing on Late Duty, is the Evil Time Warrior – none other than Mr Tempus himself.

He stands straight and strict in his well-pressed black suit and tie. He's also heavily armed with pen and clipboard ready to capture the names of his victims and rob them of their after-school-life.

Mr Tempus always sticks to the rules – so it's going to take all my skill to defeat him.

Level 2:	**Tempus the Evil Time Warrior**
Location:	**Ancient Japan**
Task:	**You have fallen through the fabric of time. You must defeat Tempus, the Evil Time Warrior, guardian of the gate, to get back on track.**

Scroll down Skills Menu

Select> *Ancient Martial Arts*

Still stylishly dressed in moody black, cyberJ faces the Evil Time Warrior and bows.

Tempus copies his move, then spreads his feet and strikes a fighting pose.

'Prepare to fight, O cyberzero!'

The Evil Warrior leads with The Praying-Mantis-Swift-Strike.

Hi-yaaa!

CyberJ blocks his move and follows through with Angry Lion-Attack.

Roaaaaar!

He knocks the Evil Time Warrior off balance but not for long. The Warrior lashes out at cyberJ with the Tiger-Claw Hack'n'Slash move.

Grrrrraaah!

At the last second cyberJ flies up high in the Soaring Dragon Somersault!

Crassshhhh!

He finishes off with a Double-Footed-Duck Kick-Flip into his enemy's back.

The Evil Time Warrior smashes into a thousand pieces of lifeless clay.

YOU WIN, CYBERJ !

GO TO THE NEXT LEVEL...

Yes...result! Mr Tempus is looking the other way – at another victim running up the street in a last-minute panic to get to school.

Now's my chance. I'm in Ancient Warrior mode and the secret is self-control and knowing when to strike. Dare I try the *Stealth-Snake-Slither* move?

I turn up my collar and crouch down low, sliding through the gates and past Tempus the Evil Time Warrior in a move as smooth as...

'Bradshaw, what's the matter? Have you got stomach ache?'

I look up to see Mr Tempus peering down at me. For a second there I almost think he looks worried. 'Er, no, sir,' I say, standing up straight. Bleep! I just lost some points. I should have said yes, but Truth is Rule Number 1 of the **Sacred Cybercode**. Someone needs to rewrite the rules.

Tempus fixes me with a hard stare and waves the other boy away, scratching down his name on the clipboard.

'Got a good reason for being late?' he asks me.

'Yes, sir,' I say. A hero.com thinks fast and I have the perfect deflecting move. 'My mum kept me in the car to tell me about your visit to our house tonight.'

I wait for him to crumble but Tempus is rock solid. 'Well, even so, you are *still* late, James Bradshaw. That's the third time this month, so it's a detention after school.'

'But, sir,' I challenge, hoping for a knock-out blow. 'Mum said I had to be home on time. She'll wonder where I am...'

'I'm glad to see you are worried about your mother's feelings but I will be able to contact her and tell her what's happened.'

He whips out his pen and carves out my name on the Ancient Clipboard of Doom.

Game Over. You lose, cyberJ!

And now it starts raining hard and there's a flash of lightning – at the same time it strikes me that Tempus and cyberM will be joining forces against me tonight.

Not only that but I'll have to face the spawn of Tempus – weird Anna – too!

As thunder explodes overhead I know that something is very wrong. This is the second level I've lost in the Game recently...and a hero.com always wins!

LEVEL 3

Nail-Blade Barricade

After school, I find myself in challenge mode. Why should I go to my detention?

If cyberM can break the rules and join forces with Mr Tempus, then I can break the rules, too. So I skip detention and advance to the next screen – home.

When Tempus and his she-spawn arrive on my territory, I am already upstairs training for the Game on my computer. I need all the practice I can get to stand up to that duo.

Then a voice-over cuts in from cyberM downstairs. It's in loud, false-polite mode. 'Jamie! We have visitors! Come on down and say hello.'

I descend into the pit of hellfire, sure that Tempus must have said something about me missing detention, but I don't think he's given the game away.

It's weird seeing your teacher sitting in your living room, sipping tea and actually smiling. It's like Blood-Fest Freddie (the hero of the game *Mega-Death Massacre*) suddenly using his blood-axe to cut flowers to take home to his Zombie-Mum. Way out of character.

The Spawn of Tempus is sitting in one of the chairs, too, looking totally weird as usual. She's got a sharp white face, spiky black hair and little black-framed glasses. She's got on lots of silver bangly-jangly things and she's dressed all in black. Well, so am I – but mine's stylish cyberhero black and hers is just sad-act black.

There's another voice-over from cyberM. 'Why don't you take Anna to your room and show her some of your computer games, Jamie? I'll call you when tea's ready.'

I figure it's better to divide the enemy and deal with them one at a time, so I follow instructions and keep in silent mode till we get to my desk.

'You choose,' I say in my bored robot

voice. Then it happens, it's like someone flicked a switch and unleashed Mighty-Motormouth Power…

'Hey, we can just talk if you like. Let's start again. I'm Anna – a palindrome! And you're Jamie, right? Funny that we're in the same year at school but we haven't spoken much. You were in the newspapers, weren't you? For being a superspy? And a rapstar? I want to be a reporter myself so I think that's really cool. You know the school mag *The Grim Times*? Well, I edit it—'

Stop! What does she mean she's a palindrome? What kind of code name is that? I want to download a stun-gun right now but I'm mesmerised by the long, metallic-silver nails at the end of her fingers.

Then she points one of her monster nail-blades right at me, '—and *you* are just what we are looking for. *You* know how to get publicity. I've got this big story coming up. We might need you to help get the message out. You're *special.* We *need* you…'

Level 3:	Nail-Blade Barricade
Location:	Cyberspace
Task:	Weird Anna wants to drain your cybersoul and get you on her side. Her claws are deadly. Resist.

Scroll down Weapons Menu

Select> *White-light cybersword*

Weird Anna blocks cyberJ, her hair stands on end in stiff black spikes and, behind her glasses, there's a cold glint in her eye.

Click!

Ten metallic claws appear at the end of her fingers.

'Welcome, cyberJ. Do you like my nail-gloss – it's slashing silver!'

She lunges at him, lashing out with flashing nails.

Smack!

CyberJ smashes his cybersword across her claws.

Five nails split off!

'Nice try, cyberJ,' says Anna. 'But a quick-fix

nail-kit will save me.'

Click! Click! Click!

'New nail-gloss!' she squeals in delight. 'Exploding Gold! Enjoy!'

Zwoosh!

A deadly cloudburst of electric-gold sparks rains down on cyberJ.

Zaapp!

He swipes at them with his cybersword, sending them flying.

Too late. His energy-meter is sinking fast.

Will he win? It's touch and go...

TIME UP. GAME OVER, CYBERJ!

'That's not fair. I've got no time!' I say, thumping the computer table.

Anna gives me a strange look. 'Oh, well, if you're too busy to help with the newspaper…'

Her face is severe now – all lines and angles, like a sharp graphic. I begin to wonder if she's real at all and remember her words earlier.

'And what did you mean, *Hello, I'm Anna – a palindrome!* What kind of alien species is that?'

She laughs. 'Not *me* – my name's a palindrome. A-N-N-A,' she spells out the letters. 'It reads the same forwards and backwards. *That's* a palindrome. Now, are you sure you won't change your mind about helping on *The Grim Times*? I think you've got a special talent—'

'Level,' I reply.

'Sorry?'

'That's a palindrome, isn't it?'

'Yes, but—'

'Radar.'

'Yes…'

'Did, dad, dud.'

'Mmm.'

'Pip, pop, poop.'

'OK,' she says. 'I think you've got it but—'

'Non!' I say happily. 'That's a French palindrome. It means *no.*'

'And your point is...?'

'Non, non, non,' I say, stuck on repeat mode.

Anna folds her arms. 'Message received loud and clear, Jamie—'

'CyberJ.'

'Yeah, whoever you are. You don't want to help with the school newspaper? Fine.' She sits down on a chair and gets something out of her bag.

I turn to the computer feeling very pleased with myself, put in a new game and wait for it to load.

'But you still might change your mind, right?'

'No! Don't you get it? I don't want to know about *The Grim Times* and your big story. Game over!'

'You're wrong.'

I look round to see Anna painting gold spots on her silver nails.

'What?'

'It's not game over, Jamie. This is just the beginning.'

Ready to play. Press Start, agrees the computer behind me.

LEVEL 4

Exit Crow Ded Hall

'What is a hero?' asks Mrs Li, our headteacher.

I put her on mute and scan round. This is the scenario – school hall, 9.15 a.m. morning assembly. And the name of the Game today is Avoid the Enemy.

'Is a hero someone who fights battles and wins medals?' Mrs Li continues.

Alert status: time to tune in – if she asks a question she might pick on someone for an answer. Some heads are nodding already. Better players of the Game, like me, keep still. We suspect a trap.

'Yes, of course that's what a hero is,' she says. 'But...and it's a very *big* but—'

There's a sudden burst of laughter at the thought of this very big butt.

'*SILENCE!*' Mrs Li gives her famous dragon roar and snuffs out the fun. Now she only has to whisper the rest. 'A hero is also someone who helps out quietly behind the scenes without making a fuss. Someone who makes a difference—'

I tune out again to work on my battle strategy. Tempus was friendly enough at tea last night but now we're in his domain and it's payback time for missing the detention. All I can do is keep out of his way and hope he'll wipe it from his memory card.

'…so we will have a special *Hero* edition of the school newspaper this term and I do hope you will put your names forward to help out.' Mrs Li's voice invades my headspace again. Another alert: the assembly is about to end. Can I make it out of the crowded hall without being seen by Tempus the Evil Time Warrior?

No contest!

A hero.com is master of stealth strategy and always wins the game. Nothing to it – I just blend in with the crowd…

Level 4:	Exit Crow Ded Hall
Location:	Busy cybercity
Task:	Tempus the Evil Time Warrior is tracking you down with his x-ray laser-eyes. Can you make it across the city to the Corridor of Freedom?

Scroll down Weapons Menu
Select> *Shield of Invisibility*
(Lasts just 30 seconds – use only in x-treme danger)
CyberJ blends in with the citizens of Crow Ded Hall making their way through the shadows to the Corridor of Freedom.
Bright stripes of light sweep over the crowds – Tempus's x-ray eyes are watching, but where is he?
Zzzzappp!
Suddenly the figure in front of cyberJ lights up like an x-ray. The flesh zaps away and only a skeleton is left standing up.
Sssigh!
Then it collapses into a pile of dust and ashes.

Zzzappp!

CyberJ dodges left and right as skeletons spring up all around him – more victims of Tempus and his deathly flesh-stripping x-ray laser-eyes.

Zzzzappp!

Now cyberJ is the only person left standing in the whole cybercity.

'Prepare to fry, O cyberJ!' sneers Tempus, looming up out of the darkness, his eyes blazing like car headlights.

Click!

CyberJ activates the Shield of Invisibility and buys 30 seconds of time...

'Thirty seconds you have been standing there, James Bradshaw, when I clearly asked everyone to sit down before they are dismissed from assembly.' Mrs Li's voice cuts in.

I look around to find hundreds of eyes all looking up at me from smug, smiling, *sitting-down* students. Something tells me my Shield of Invisibility is just not working.

'Really, it's like you're in a world of your own!

Now, sit down please. And report to my office after this.'

As I crumple into my chair, I feel a pair of eyes upon me that seem to strip me to my cybersoul. Tempus appears on stage and he's blazing with anger.

Who pressed his buttons? Then I get it. Mrs Li has just taken away his controls! If I have to see her after assembly then he can't grab me for missing the detention, can he?

Yes! I win...er, I think. The downside is that I am *still* in trouble with Mrs Li, but don't forget my lightning reflexes and multi-skills – she doesn't stand a chance.

Proceed to the Dragon's Den

Five minutes later, I'm standing Mrs Li's office preparing my strategy. I straighten my school tie and set my smile on *lock*. Time for a charm attack.

'Mrs Li will see you now,' says her secretary.

My jaws are aching but I keep up the smile and enter the Dragon's Den.

'Ah, James Bradshaw, I wanted to speak to you this week...please, take a seat.' She's in Crouching-Dragon-Pretend-Friendly mode. Not a wisp of smoke escapes her throat as she talks.

She picks up some papers from her desk and looks at them for a minute. 'Yes, I've had some reports from your teachers about your strange behaviour. This morning, in assembly, I could see why.'

I'm still locked on *smile*. Now I cross my legs and put my head on one side. The classic *How very interesting, do tell me more* pose.

'Let me share a few phrases from these reports with you. *Spaced out...not playing the game...distracted.*'

She stops and a spiral of smoke escapes from one nostril. 'Less than satisfactory, is it not?'

'No,' I say, nodding... 'I mean, Yes,' I say, shaking my head. 'I mean...er can you reload the question?'

She takes off her glasses and gives me a hard look. 'My point exactly,' she says.

'And on top of all this, Mr Tempus tells me that you missed a detention yesterday.'

A shadow suddenly falls across the room. Is there no escape from the Evil Time Warrior? He's here in spirit even if he's not here in body. And I wouldn't be too sure of that, either. I bet he's got an Invisibility Shield of his own.

I start to scan round me, into the darkest corners and even look over my shoulder, just in case.

'Jamie, pay attention!' the dragon roars. I sit up straight. Now I know how she got to be headteacher. I think she just burned off one of my eyebrows.

'What you need is to take on some responsibility. You heard what I said in assembly this morning – well, *some* of it at least?'

I nod and smile, breaking the **Sacred Cybercode of Truth**. To be honest, I haven't got a clue. All that data has already been deleted from my memory banks.

'And you will help out?'

I nod again. Whatever it is, it's got to be better than a week of after-school detentions.

Mrs Li smiles and glows a little bit, 'Well done, Jamie. I knew you'd see sense.'

She starts scribbling on a pad of paper. 'We'll send a letter home, explaining that you will be busy after school for the next few weeks. You'll be helping with *The Grim Times* newspaper – Anna Tempus is in charge so she'll fill you in. There's a meeting tomorrow, I think.'

Anna Tempus? After school? Newspaper?

Aaaagbbb!

This isn't how the Game works out.

Reboot!

Can I play this level over again?

LEVEL 5

Evil Eye

Nooo! I've tried to switch off and shut down but there's no way to reboot the Game and play the level over. I'm programmed to meet Anna – Queen of the Palindromes and editor of *The Grim Times* – in five minutes.

Time has moved too fast and here I am, my feet tapping along the empty corridors after school. Everyone else has escaped but I have a date with Fate in the Resource Centre (aka the school library).

At least I know that *The Grim Times* group is a multi-player outfit. There was a notice about it on the School Council Board and five or six have signed up.

My strategy is to take a back seat, save my valuable energy levels and let the others do all the work. I'm also going to keep Anna at arm's length – she's not going to nail me down again.

The Resource Centre is straight ahead. I push open the Door of Destiny and scan round for enemy activity.

Anna is sitting at the head of a table looking busy and making some notes. She looks up when I come in and tries to disarm me with a friendly smile. 'Jamie – what a surprise! Come and sit down, I'm so glad you decided to help us.'

She points at the chairs with her dangerous nail-blades.

'What do you mean *us*? All the chairs are empty, Anna. So does everyone else have an Invisibility Shield or what?'

She sighs and drums her nail-blades on the table – they've got eyes painted on them today. 'I was expecting *more* people but Grace had to go to the dentist. Josh, Andy and Imran had football practice and Laura's away—'

'Oh well, we'll just have to wait and see if anyone else turns up,' I say, walking over to a computer and switching it on.

'No, we have to go out and cover that big story! I've left a message with the librarian in case anyone arrives late.'

I reach out for the headphones so I can block out her voice while I surf the net but she gets there first and grabs them off the table.

'And we have to go *now*,' she adds. Then she stabs at the **Off** button on the computer and her nail-blades flash dangerously.

Level 5:	**Evil Eye**
Location:	**Cyberdome**
Task:	**Anna Tempus is trying to take control of your mind and body. If she touches you with all of her evil eyes you die!**

Anna Tempus spreads out her ten finger-blades with ten evil eyes painted on them. The eyes blink as if alive.

'Night, night, cyberJ. Sleep well!'

She waves her nail-blades around in hypno-mode and then makes a jab at cyberJ.

He springs back just a second too late. A tiny cut on his left hand leaves him frozen to the spot.

Now she returns for the kill. She's ready to slice'n'dice him with all ten nail-blades!
'Surrender, cyberJ. You've got no option.'
Anna's arms start whirring round and round, her nails whistling through the air like a thousand helicopter blades.
Whrrrrrrrrrrrrrrrr!
CyberJ tries to chop, twist, hover, back flip.
Nothing.
She leaps at him and...

'*Noooooo!*'

'Jamie, be quiet, this is a library! And what do you mean, no? Mrs Li said you agreed to help out instead of doing detention. We're doing an interview so we can take a digital voice recorder, or a digital camera. They're brand new. You're good with technical stuff. What shall we choose?'

So Anna's trying the Flattery Strategy is she? Her tactics are so obvious! Still, the camera and voice recorder are very tempting.

'Select both options,' I say, taking them from her. 'So where's the interview and what's the scenario?'

Go to Next Screen

The scenario turns out to be a business estate a bus ride away on the other side of town. It's all newly built in brick and metal with a security fence around it and a sign that reads:

Nova World – Designs for the Future

Anna checks her notes. 'This is him – our local hero,' she says. 'He was on the radio the other day. He said he had big plans for the town park – he sounded perfect for a feature in *The Grim Times*.'

She presses the button on the gate and speaks into the intercom. 'It's Anna Tempus and…er a friend. We've come to interview Mr Nova.'

The gate buzzes and swings open. '*Proceed straight ahead to Level 3*,' says an electronic voice.

Our feet clank on the metallic floor as we approach the elevator ahead. Everything in the building is colour co-ordinated in grey, black or bloodbath red. I feel so at home here – it's like being inside that new computer game *Urban Chic Shoot-out*, except that there are no people, aliens or ferocious predators.

Anna presses a button next to the elevator. '*Doors opening*,' says an electronic voice. We enter and she presses for Level 3. '*Doors closing*,' says the voice.

'You don't say...' I mutter, getting annoyed – where's the mute button when you need it? 'Hey, Anna are you sure Mr Nova really exists? Maybe we'll walk into his office and we'll just get this electronic voice going, "*Welcome. You are now shaking my hand. You are now yawning your heads off. I am now scratching my butt—*"'

'Jamie!'

'Make that cyberJ,' I say, holding the digital camera in front of me and snapping a quick photo of Anna's shocked face.

I play it back and show her the image.

'That's terrible!' she says but she's laughing, too. 'Promise to delete it, please?'

'I'll think about it,' I say as the elevator stops and we both join in with its voice. '*Level 3. Doors opening.*'

As we stand in another cold metallic corridor, Anna switches to serious mode for a minute. 'We haven't seen a soul since we got here, this place gives me the creeps,' she whispers. 'You know I'm glad you came with me, Jamie.'

'CyberJ,' I say. 'And you know what? I kinda like this futuristic, urban, techno-design.'

She looks at me open-mouthed. Those words are from the back of a computer game package in a shop on Grimly High Street but I don't tell her. Always keep your opponent guessing.

Then a door swings open in front of us and a voice says, 'Glad you like the design, cyberJ. Please enter and then you can find out if I do exist, after all.'

Anna and I look at each other as we realise that the elevator has hidden extra features – it can listen as well as speak. How else would Mr Nova know what I said about him?

'*Going down. Doors closing. Watch your backs,*' says the elevator as a parting shot.

Now there's no escape.

We walk towards the open door ahead of us as if someone else is pressing our controls.

LEVEL 6

Nu-Look Cybercity

At first it seems that my theory is right and Mr Nova doesn't exist at all. The room is filled with hardware – banks of computers, scanners and a photocopier, but no sign of a human.

Suddenly the computer screensavers ahead of us flicker and burst into life. Music blasts out and a message scrolls across the screen:

Welcome, Anna and cyberJ!

Then the letters start jigging around to the music.

'This guy is some kind of control-freak,' I mutter to Anna. 'Try not to look impressed.'

Too late. She's already clapping and cooing, 'Ooh how did he do that? It's very good!'

Suddenly a figure jumps out from the back of the room – as surprising as an on-screen pop-up – and Anna shrieks up a storm.

He springs towards us and holds out his hand. 'Hey, it's OK. I'm Nova – not a virtual image or a voiceover but in the flesh.'

We shake hands – he's a small, wiry man with a shaved head and tinted specs. He's wearing a sharp black suit and moves around a lot in a jerky way, like a badly programmed animated figure.

'Welcome to my world,' he says proudly, opening his arms out to include the computers, like they're part of the family.

Anna suddenly gets brisk and business-like.

'Thank you, Mr Nova—'

'Nova – Mr is so out-dated, don't you think?'

'Well, er…I never really thought about it. So…Nova, what exactly is your world? Tell us about it, please.'

'Is it OK to record the interview, Nova?' I cut in.

He nods.

Press play:

Nova:	*My world is the interface between dreams and reality. You picture something in your head, plan it on the computer screen, then make it happen! I was born and raised in Grimly but my talent with computers took me to the United States of America. That's where I developed my cutting edge, Computer-Aided Town-Planning And Design System – CATPADS.*
Anna:	*I believe you were there for ten years, Nova. So why did you come back?*
Nova:	*I guess it's true what they say, there's no place like home. A part of me wants to make my mark here, give something back, you know?*
Anna:	*Do you have any plans for how to do that?*
Nova:	*Well, as a matter of fact, I'm working*

on a project right now. The local council has asked me to show some designs at the MAKE GRIMLY GREAT planning meeting next month. Let me give you a little preview…

Press stop.

He double-clicks a touch pad and a 3D townscape appears on the screen.

'Hey, look!' I say. 'That's Grimly High Street and there's our school and the park and—'

He double-clicks again to show a slick high-tech cityscape with some high-rise glass-fronted buildings on the skyline.

'This could be Grimly in ten years from now,' he says proudly and highlights a building near the school.

'Let's start here. This park is a prime spot for a sports centre. Top class facilities, swimming pool, gym, games areas. Then—'

But I don't hear any more. This is the Future – from computer simulation to the next generation. And I can't wait. I want it *now*…

Level 6:	Nu-look Cybercity
Location:	You choose!
Task:	Destroy an old town and build your own dream cityscape.

Scroll down Weapons Menu

Select> Explodaball and chain

CyberJ wears his surprise-attack jet-pack and flies through the sky. He looks down over small-town Grimly. It needs a maxi-power makeover and he's the one to do it.

CyberJ looks through his shades and locks on target. First to go is the school. What else? He takes the explodaball from his attack-pack and rotates it in circles on its chain. Faster and faster it whizzes, round and round over his head. Then he lets it go—

Boom!

The ball explodes on impact. *Flash! Bang! Crash!* No school. Not a classroom, not a science lab, not even a crisp packet.

CyberJ stands in the middle of the cleared landscape and pulls out his hand-held

instant virtual-build device. Now what to replace his school with? He flips though the on-screen design options:

CyberJ Skatepark

CyberJ Sports Centre

CyberJ Games Arcade

It's like choosing the toppings for a pizza – sometimes you just want 'em all. Now, where to start?

'And when will you make a start with these changes, Nova?' Anna's voice sounds suddenly high-pitched and tense.

'Oh, I get bored fast,' he says, double-clicking and switching screens. 'So, when they give it the green light, we activate the plans in a nanosecond.'

'Hey, I forgot to switch on again,' I say. 'Can we repeat the interview from—'

'No, Jamie. We've heard enough. Let's go.' Anna grabs the voice recorder off me before I can block her.

'That's too bad, I wanted to show you some of the other plans I have for Grimly—'

'Yeah, cool. I'd like to hear that,' I say as Anna moves towards the door.

'Sorry, Nova. We'll miss the bus if we don't go now. Come *on*, Jamie.'

'But there'll be another bus in twenty minutes...'

Too late – Nova's got distracted and starts surfing the net. Meanwhile, Anna's out the door and halfway across the hall.

'*Doors opening, going down*,' says a familiar electronic voice outside. There doesn't seem to be any other option.

When we get in the elevator I'm ready for a face-off. 'What was all that about, Anna? Why'd you pull the plug on the interview just as it was getting interesting?'

Anna starts making cutting noises to her throat. Then she whispers, 'Tell you later, Jamie. Walls have ears, remember?'

'Yeah, well it's a pity girls don't have brains.'

She turns her back on me and we leave in silence but I don't care. What gives her the right to take over the Game like this?

Well, if she thinks I'm working with her again

she can forget it. She can't even get my name right – it's cyberJ!

And from now on this hero.com is operating in single-player mode.

LEVEL 7

Cybercity Bomb Blitz

Anna comes up to me at dinner-time next day and she's no joystick, I can tell you. In fact she's in full-on misery mode and acting the control-freak as usual.

'Emergency meeting, *The Grim Times.* Resource Centre after school. Operation Kickback,' she says. I have no idea what she's talking about – perhaps her words are encrypted.

The problem is that gamers are naturally curious, so I go along to the meeting to see what she has to say about Nova. I still don't know why she cut the interview short – maybe she wants to reload and try again.

When I get to the Resource Centre it looks like this is a multi-player set-up for a change. *The Grim Times* group have put down their Invisibility Shields and about six of them are sitting round the table.

I open the door to find Anna in megamouth mode already. 'Jamie, I was just telling everyone about Nova and his terrible plans—'

'Oh yeah? What terrible plans were those, then?' I say, dodging the attack with a clever use of Question Tactics.

'But you were there! You heard him say he'd build on the town park—'

'That's right. He's going to MAKE GRIMLY GREAT. He's going to build a sports centre with a swimming pool and a gym and—'

'It's not *what* he's building that's wrong, it's *where* he's building that's wrong. OK, Grimly needs a good sports centre but there are other places on the edge of town. Why build on a park?'

'Park? How can you call that a park? It's overgrown wasteland! You'll be lucky if a blade of grass fights its way up through all the litter and dog poo—'

'But that's no reason to build on it. Jamie, Grimly Park is the only green space we've got left in town. *The Grim Times* is not going to stand by and see Nova take it away. That's why I called us together today. This is an emergency!'

'Yeah? And what can *we* do? You heard Nova – he's taking the plans to a council meeting next week. They're not going to listen to us!'

'Well, we've got to tell people what's happening. A sports centre means more traffic – and that's a hot issue…'

Anna's in full-on freak-out mode now. She's stabbing the air with her fingers to back up her words – and today her nail-blades are flaming red…

Level 7:	Cybercity Bomb Blitz
Location:	Nu-look cyberJ City
Task:	Anna Tempus, Queen of the Palindromes, plans to wipe out your dreamscape. Prepare for an all-out air attack.

Red alert! Red alert! Enemy forces approaching. Take cover!

There! Hovering above the *CyberJ Games Arcade* (former site of the old Grimly High School) is a vast army of spaceships.

Sploosh! Sploosh! Sploosh!

Nooo! It's a nail-gloss bomb-blitz and the Games Arcade takes a direct hit!

Sizzling red-hot nail-gloss splurges over the entire building coating it in a rock-hard, diamond-finish shell. The army moves on and more locations take a hit.

Sploosh! – the CyberJ Football Stadium

Sploosh! – the CyberJ Nightclub

Sploosh! – the CyberJ Skatepark

All victims of the flaming-red bomb-fest. All now totally glossy and totally useless!

CyberJ scrolls down his Weapons Menu.

Select weapon> ***Automatic pump-action anti-aircraft gun***

Select ammo> ***Deadly acid nail-polish remover***

CyberJ yells a war cry to the sky...

'Hasta la vista, Anna, I'm gonna clean up round here!'

'Sorry, Jamie? You're muttering to yourself again. Clean up? What d'you mean?'

'Maybe he means we could clean up the town park,' says one of *The Grim Times* group.

'No chance! It would take an army to do that,' says another.

'Jamie, you're a genius!' Anna's eyes are shining like spaceships in the dark. 'We can run a clean-up campaign and tell the whole town about it.'

And before I know what's happening she's giving orders and taking control again. 'Let's have a vote. All *The Grim Times* group members in favour of starting a *Clean-up the Park* campaign, put your hands up.'

All hands go up.

'That's it then. We're all agreed. A clean sweep!' she says, laughing at her own joke.

'But Jamie didn't vote,' one task force member dares to challenge.

'That's because he made the proposal,' Anna shoots back in a swift counter-attack.

Yet again she's doing all the talking for me. And as usual she's way off course. I was waiting for the chance to vote NO.

'Right, I declare the meeting over – we've got lots to think about. Let's get together at the same time tomorrow to make an action plan.'

The others drift off but I stand my ground. I'm ready to download, offload and reload my best insults onto mega-mouth Anna.

I draw breath, ready to let rip. Nothing can stop me now...but then she whips something out of her bag – lip gloss!

Red Alert – Secret Weapon! What's she going to do with it?

There's some writing on it – **Strawberry and...***shoot!* I can't see the rest and it might give me a clue.

Stand back. She's taking off the lid! Anything could happen. Now she's running the stuff over her mouth and it activates her speaker system.

'Oh, I'm so glad you're still on our side, Jamie. For a minute there I thought you'd joined up with Nova! I'm sorry I doubted you.'

Double Red Alert! She's got her blood-fest red nails on my arm. Now she's puckering up and kissing me on the cheek!

...*Mmm.* **Strawberry and a hint of mint**. Yes – she gets *that* close.

It's a surprise attack and my defences are weakening!

LEVEL 8

Zombie Invasion!

I get home from school feeling dazed and confused.

The Game is getting more and more complex and I'm not sure whose side I'm on now.

Shall I join forces with Anna and *The Grim Times* group to save the park? Or shall I side with Nova and his bid to build a sports centre?

CyberM's not back yet – so I rush upstairs, pull the curtains and retreat to the private, twilight world of my bedroom and my cuddly computer.

After crashing cars, blowing stuff up and smashing alien butt, I feel so much better.

Just as I'm saving a game, the front door clicks. It signals the return of cyberM which means it's time to refuel. This is her supermarket night, so I'm looking forward to unlocking some extra bonus eat-treats from her shopping bags.

As I open my bedroom door I hear the low

murmur of voices. My quick reflexes put me on stealth mode and stop me pressing the light switch. Instead I move silently to the top of the stairs and look down. In the half-dark I can see two figures – one is cyberM and the other is the shadowy shape of Tempus the Evil Time Warrior!

Not only is this a second invasion of my cyberspace but, even as I am looking, the talking stops and something truly horrific happens.

Tempus downloads the shopping bags and takes cyberM into his arms like a zombie hugging its prey.

Level 8:	**Zombie Invasion**
Location:	**Nu-look cyberJ City**
Task:	**Tempus the Evil Time Warrior has evolved. Now he's Tempus THE EVIL ZOMBIE Time Warrior! He's leading an army of zombies into your city. They eat your brains and turn you into the Undead. Stop him invading your home!**

CyberJ runs through the streets of his city in a desperate race against time.

Behind him stalks a tribe of zombie citizens with pale clammy skin and mesmerised eyes, chanting,

Brain Feast!

Brain Feast!

Brain Feast!

CyberJ dodges left, right, up, down, gets home and slams the door behind him. CyberM is safe upstairs.

YOU WIN. GO TO NEXT LEVEL.

Smash! Bash! Crash!

CyberJ is home but the Zombies break down the front door! He stands his ground in a frantic face-off.

Scroll down Skills Menu

Select> *spin kick, ninja slam, twisting hammer-blow*

CyberJ uses every trick in the book.

Kick! Slam! Splat!

It's bone-crunching fun but zombies feel no pain. As soon as they shoot out of the door they get up again and start over.

He glances over his shoulder to check on cyberM.

Crash!

Nooo! At that very second Tempus the Evil Zombie Time Warrior smashes the bathroom window, snatches cyberM up into his arms and...

Noooo! I can't look any more... Tempus and cyberM! It's not just a peck on the cheek – it's a lip-on-lip direct hit! *Yeuch, it's a total slobber-fest.* More sick and disgusting than any 18+ computer game!

This breaks every rule of the **Sacred Cybercode**. I feel betrayed. It takes the Game onto a totally different level. This is War!

And now I'm in dual shock because I suddenly remember my last contact with Anna. OK, so it wasn't a lip-on-lip direct hit but it was a close thing. One false move and it might have been full-on! What is it with Tempus and his spawn? Why can't they use legal moves instead of cheats?

At least now I'm wise to their game. They want to drain our brains and make us into zombies who do whatever they want. Then they'll invade our home and completely take over!

But they are forgetting that a hero.com always wins, no matter what sneaky, underhand tricks the enemy uses. Now it's time to rethink my Game Plan.

'Jamie, come and eat!' cyberM calls from downstairs.

I move slowly and scan the whole house for enemy activity but, thankfully, the Evil Zombie Time Warrior has gone.

In the kitchen cyberM acts as if nothing happened. 'We've got pepperoni pizza – your favourite,' she smiles. 'And there's some chocolate-chip ice cream to follow.'

'Uh-huh,' I grunt, checking her skin to see if it looks grey and clammy – the first sign of zombification.

'Yes, I bought you a treat because Mr Tempus heard from Anna that you're really helping out with *The Grim Times.* He says you're really changing…'

Not into the brain-drained zombie he wants, I think as cyberM passes me the pizza. Then I look into her eyes which are big and dark and glassy.

The eyes of the Undead.

LEVEL 9

S.O.S.

◆ CyberJ, can you hear me?

◆ Yes, who are you? Where are you? I can't see. Everything is dark.

◆ You do not need your eyes to see inside your cybersoul. Tell me, what do you fear?

◆ I fear the Undead. They're closing in all around me. They have a secret weapon – the Kiss of Death! It comes in more than one flavour...

◆ CyberJ, you must not allow yourself to be distracted. Focus on the Ultimate Level. What is your aim in the Game?

◆ I want to be a hero – a hero.com. I want...to fulfil my destiny, to fight for what is right!

◆ Remember the words of the Sacred

Cybercode. For it is written that sometimes a hero must walk alone.

- **Yes, but–**
- **The time is now, cyberJ. now Now NOW.**

'Jamie, I said it's time to get up now!' The shadows merge into one dark shape which looms over me and grabs my shoulders.

'No! Gerrroff! Leave me alone!' I open my eyes to see cyberM spring back in surprise.

'Now look, Jamie. I know you're tired but please control yourself. It's not as if I'm the enemy!'

Oh yes you are, I think, *but you don't even know it.*

'Mmph, bad dream,' I mumble to cover up my thoughts – perhaps zombies can read your mind. Anyway, it's not her fault she's now officially Life Impaired.

'Maybe I shouldn't buy that pizza again if it gives you nightmares.'

'No, I'm fine, really. And you ate it too, how do *you* feel?'

'Very well, as a matter of fact. You know I was

so pleased when Frank…er, Mr Tempus, told me about your Clean-up Campaign because—'

'Is that clock right?' I cut in fast. She's trying to brainwash me with the thoughts of Tempus and his spawn but I'm wise to her tricks.

'Oops, must dash, I've got an early morning appointment at the salon! Remind me to tell you about the park tonight, OK? Now, can you get yourself ready, lock up and get to school on time?'

'I've done it before, haven't I?' I say, reaching for my clothes.

Advance to next screen

But today is different. Dark clouds are brooding in the sky as I join the line of Grimly students trudging up the hill to school where Tempus the Evil Zombie Time Warrior patrols the gates.

We all look the same in our black school coats with their red Grimly High badges. Our skins are grey in the morning light, our eyes are glazed and dull from days of study and homework. Someone needs to Save Our Souls.

Level 9:	S.O.S.
Location:	Grim Reaper CyberSchool
Task:	Tempus the Evil Zombie Time Warrior is stealing students' souls by ripping off their school badges. Stop him!

Scroll down Skills Menu

Select> *hawk-hover/eagle-swoop*

CyberJ hovers hawk-eyed over the city streets, ready for action. Down below an innocent student strolls towards the school gates.

Swissssh!

Tempus the Evil Zombie Time Warrior sweeps out of the main doors and across the school yard like a bat out of Hell.

Aaaagh! The student freezes with fear.

Tempus reaches out with bony fingers as cyberJ dives out of the sky in eagle-strike mode.

Swoooop! Snatch!

CyberJ grabs the school badge – just

seconds before Tempus gets there. He holds the badge up high.

Badoom! Badoom! Badoom!

It glows bright red and starts beating like a heart.

Bleep!

One bar lights up on the Soul-o-meter.

One soul saved, hundreds to go. Look out cyberJ. The clock is ticking...

'Look out, Tempus about,' Imran warns me and sure enough here he comes, stalking out of the school gates, checking his watch. Suddenly we all start walking faster as if brainwashed already.

'Ah, Bradshaw. I just want a quick word with you.'

Nooo! Tempus is moving towards me and he's armed to the teeth with…teeth. Yes, he's smiling. At *me*! He's never used that tactic before and it's horrifying.

'I just wanted to thank you for the help you've given Anna.'

Everyone is looking at me. I'm not surprised.

Tempus is chatting to me as if we were on the same side, not mortal enemies.

'With your help she thinks the game will be up for that designer...er, what's his name, Rover?'

'Nova.'

'That's it. And I know I don't need to remind you about the meeting after school today. Jamie...Jamie, where are you going?'

'Sorry, sir. I just remembered something. Won't be long,' I say. Then I turn around and put on some speed.

'Bradshaw, come back!' he shouts, but I screen him out.

It's true, I have just remembered something: the voice in my dream saying, *Sometimes a hero must walk alone* – it was Nova!

Suddenly school is not an option – all those lost, grey souls walking to their doom day after day. We're all burnt out. We need to be recharged. Anna, Tempus and the rest of the brainwashed zombie-tribe are all wrong. We need a sports centre, not a patch of land that is dog-poo heaven. We need to MAKE GRIMLY GREAT!

Someone needs to warn Nova. Someone needs to be a hero.com to stand up and fight for what is right.

CyberJ, your time has come!

LEVEL 10

Super Nova

So I replay the level Anna and I failed the other day and head back to Nova World. There isn't a bus around so I walk. No, delete that last word, I'm running so fast it's like teleporting and I end up at Nova's gate five seconds before I set off.

Now to repeat the same moves. I press the buzzer and enter my name-code: 'CyberJ to speak to Nova please.'

'*Enter*' says the electro-voice.

The elevator greets me like an old friend as I walk into the building and tickle its buttons.

'*Welcome. Ground Floor, doors closing.*'

It pauses for a while and then adds, '*Level 3, doors opening.*'

'Yeah, I know. See ya later, elevator.' I wave as I cross the hall to Nova's office.

And here's Nova bouncing out of his chair,

his glasses glinting in the glow of his computer screen.

'Hey, if it isn't my young friend cyberJ. Take a seat.'

I sit down, suddenly mute.

'So what brings you here during school time – another interview?'

'They're trying to stop you!' The words just pop up like an on-screen alert.

Nova pauses and looks at me. 'Run that by me again, cyberJ. Who—'

'The zom…er, I mean Anna, the girl who came here with me the other day. She's working with *The Grim Times* group, they're going to—'

'Stop right there, cyberJ,' Nova interrupts me before I can finish. 'I want to thank you for coming to warn me – you're a micro-chip off the old block, aren't you?'

'But—?'

'Yeah, your dad was a real pal to me at school. I haven't told anyone this before but he used to stand up for me. We were both bullied, you know. Your dad because of…well…'

'His colour,' I say.

'You got it. He was the only black kid in school and kids can be cruel sometimes. Things change though, don't they?'

I nod. We're running way off track now, but I'm curious. 'So why were *you* bullied?'

He laughs. 'I was a weedy little swot, nerd, geek – whatever they call it these days. He used to say to me – walk tall, think big. I was sorry to hear he…'

'It was his heart. I was only three, so I can't remember him much.'

'Well, remember his words then. Walk tall, think big. Now relax, there's no problem. The sports centre's safe. Your friend can't do a thing.'

He leans back in his chair and looks totally in control of his game. This man's a true hero.com. Now I know I was right to come here. 'But she knows—'

'Don't worry. Even if your friend knows she won't find any proof.'

Now the Game takes on a new twist. When I said *Anna knows*, I meant she knows how to get things done.

'Proof?' I repeat, like a stupid cyberparrot.

He taps the side of his nose. 'My lawyer dug up an old legal document that stops the park from being built on. Some royal decree calling it *common land* was filed away in London somewhere. Lucky for us he found it before anyone else did. Now it's history! Deleted! There's nothing that money can't do,' he laughs.

'Deleted?'

'Listen,' he switches to serious all of a sudden. 'You want this sports centre, don't you?'

I nod.

'Well, you're a gamer, cyberJ. Haven't you ever used illegal cheats?'

'Yeah,' I say, my voice almost a whisper, 'but that was in a game.'

Nova stands up now. His voice gets louder and he's waving his arms around. He's a small guy but he suddenly seems to fill the room. 'This is no game, cyberJ. I want that sports centre slap bang in the centre of town with my name on it in massive letters that light up at night. That'll show those kids from school. Think big, that's what Nova does. Someone should have told them: *Be nice to geeks cos when you grow up you'll end up working for one.*'

Then he starts laughing like a power-crazed maniac.

Level 10:	**Super Nova**
Location:	**Nova World**
Task:	**Nova is about to evolve. His alter-ego is Evil. Stop him!**

CyberJ and Nova stand in a face-off.

Nova:	**Welcome to my world cyberJ. Are you with me or against me?**
CyberJ:	**Er...**
Nova:	**Too late! You had your chance. Now see, hear and fear! THINK BIG – ACTIVATE SUPER-NOVA!**

Nova presses a button on his cyberbelt.

Bang!

His legs and arms grow, like huge trees.

Boom!

His chest inflates like an emergency airbag.

Crash!

Massive slabs of metal fly through the air and cover his giant body and head in shining armour.

Flash!

A huge sword flies into his fist.

He towers over tiny cyberJ – defenceless in his long black coat.

Nova: **(*evil voice sfx*) I WILL REPEAT THE QUESTION...**

'So, are you with me or against me, cyberJ?' Nova's eyes flash dangerously behind his sharp specs.

Now it clicks. This isn't about MAKING GRIMLY GREAT – it's about making Nova great. For him this is pay-back time from when he was the little kid at school.

'With you,' I whisper, breaking the **Sacred Cybercode of Truth**.

'Of course you are. You're a gamer, like me. If you wanna win you gotta break the rules. It's not as if anyone gets hurt, is it?'

I shake my head.

Nova checks his watch. 'Time's up. Nice talking to you – strictly off the record, of course. I know you won't repeat it. Nova's a good friend but a bad enemy. Remember that.'

He presses a button and the elevator speaks. '*Level 3, doors open, going down.*'

Now it doesn't sound friendly any more.

It sounds like a killer robot on a bad day.

LEVEL 11

Meltdown

It's nearly lunchtime when I'm ejected from Nova world. Now the Game is more mega-complex than ever.

I *do* want a sports centre but Nova's taken cheating onto a whole new level. He's paid money to destroy a legal document – that's breaking the law! I can't deal with it right now and I can't face the trouble-fest if I go back to school either.

There's only one sure-fire strategy to take my mind off things. So I take off my school tie, turn up my coat collar, put on my shades and escape into a games shop on the High Street.

After an afternoon of crashing, bashing and slashing I've blocked out everything else. By the time I exit the shop I'm suffering severe cyber-injuries – sore thumbs, blurry vision and brain drain (painful but not life-threatening).

After a slow walk home I settle down for my usual hour slumped in front of the TV before cyberM gets in...

But only seconds later she sweeps though the door, straight into the front room and clicks the TV off.

'Jamie, I need to talk to you.'

'Hey, I was watching that!' I protest. 'It just got to the bit where—'

'How was school today, Jamie?'

Alert status – she knows. Then again, maybe I'm getting a false message? Time for a tactical game.

'Er...OK – same as ever,' I say. Well, it's not exactly breaking the **Sacred Cybercode of Truth**, is it? I mean, the school is still standing as far as I know.

'And what about the after-school meeting about the park?

'Oooh!' I say, banging my head with my hand and playing the drama strategy. 'Was that tonight? I *knew* I'd forgotten something.'

'Jamie, stop playing games with me! This is serious. When Frank phoned to say you'd walked out of school this morning I was worried sick! He told me not to panic – to wait and see if you'd turn up at the meeting after school, but you didn't. So *where* were you?'

'Frank? Who's Frank?'

'Oh, you know…Mr Tempus. He even had to inform the police—'

'Why? What's it got to do with them? He's always invading my space. I wish he'd leave me alone!'

'Jamie! He's worried about you and so am I. He's told me you're in all sorts of trouble at school…I don't know you any more. You don't tell me anything. It's as if you're in a world of your own…'

'Yeah? Well maybe that's because you're too busy with your dearest, darling Frank!'

'Jamie, don't speak to me like that. Go to your room.'

I shoot out of my chair and stand in front of her ready for a face-off. 'No. Why should I? You can't make me.'

And suddenly it's true. We're standing eyeball to eyeball and I'm as tall as cyberM. When did that happen?

CyberM lowers her voice and speaks slowly. 'Jamie, go to your room. You need to calm down.'

But I can't. I'm in overdrive. 'And don't think he's going to move in and start bossing me around, either. He's not my dad!'

CyberM flinches and I know I've scored a point – then she hits back. 'Well, if your dad could see you like this, Jamie, how d'you think he'd feel? He'd be so—'

'Shut *up*!'

And now something deep inside is triggered off and I totally lose control.

Level 11:	**Meltdown**
Location:	**The Void**
Task:	**Use every trick in the book to crush the enemy!**

The Enemy is all around, closing in. Unseen but all-powerful. CyberJ unleashes max-volcano power.

Lava Leap

Exploding headbutt

Pyroclastic punch

There's no stopping him now.

'Jamie, stop!'

A voice-over freeze-frames me with my fists raised. What's happening? CyberM's face is greyed-out in front of me. I'm in conflict mode. Is it too late to stop myself…

Slam!

Ouch, that hurt! A red hot flame of pain spurts up my arm as my fist slams into concrete. At the very last minute I turned away from cyberM and diverted the moves to the wall. But it just beat me and won maximum points.

'Jamie, go to your room.' CyberM's voice is a harsh whisper. Her eyes are black holes in a face drained of blood.

And this time I do as she says because if I stay, I'm afraid of what my next move will be. I thunder upstairs and crash into my room.

Slam!

Now I'm punching pillows and kicking and shouting until my energy meter runs out. Then I fall onto my bed like a wounded warrior. I feel empty but my eyes are hot and stinging and I'm shaking all over.

The Game is out of control and I want to shut it down and erase the last minutes from my memory card.

But I can't.

I can't stop or click **Pause** or press **Escape**.

Suddenly I don't want to move up to the next level. It's too difficult and I've lost my way. The picture is blurry and I don't even know which character I'm supposed to be.

Am I a hero or a *zero*?

LEVEL 12

No Game

Next morning I hear cyberM moving around downstairs. There's no *Hurry up – you're late for school!* voice-over so I guess she's switched on mute because of last night.

I get up and dressed fast, hoping to gain some badly-needed points on the cyberM-o-meter.

The strategy fails when I walk into the kitchen. CyberM takes one look at me and says, 'You don't need to wear your school uniform today, Jamie. You've been suspended.'

'Why? Wha—?' I stutter like a broken printer.

'This came in the post,' she says, handing me a letter.

Grimly High School *<u>Fixed Term Exclusion</u>*

Pupil Name: James Bradshaw

Dear Mrs Bradshaw,

I regret to inform you that I have had to exclude your child from school for one day. The reason for this is that he broke the rules today. He walked out of school and refused to return when a teacher requested that he do so.

Please fill in the tear-off slip below to acknowledge receipt of this letter.

Yours sincerely,

Mrs Li
Headteacher

Seeing it set out in black and white is a shock. The Game isn't fun to play any more. I want to forget about it and get off to school like a normal 3D person.

It's time to get real but I can't. As far as school goes I've been wiped off the screen.

I sit down at the kitchen table. 'I'm sorry Mum. Yesterday…well, I just had to go and see Nova about the park—'

Mum sits down too. 'Jamie, I know you feel strongly about the park. I shouldn't have said what I did. In fact I know your dad would be proud of you—'

'Yeah?'

'Yes, he loved that park. The heart and lungs of Grimly, he used to call it. He played football there as a boy and that's where he trained the Under Eleven football team every Sunday morning. All this was before you were born – and before it was left to run wild, of course…'

'But—'

'Just let me finish, Jamie. As I said, you feel strongly about the park and you're at an age now where you've got strong feelings about lots of things. Look at you, you're growing up so fast. You're as tall as me now, aren't you?'

So she noticed it, too, last night. I nod, trying to block out the flashback.

'Well – I don't want to sound like a cheesy film script here but *power is nothing without control.* You've got so much going for you, Jamie, but you have to learn to channel your energy and not lose it. Like last night…'

I nod. Speaking is no longer an option. There's some kind of block in my throat.

CyberM shakes her head sadly. 'Sometimes I think you are your own worst enemy.'

We both sit for a few seconds like someone's pressed **Pause** and frozen the moment.

Then she starts up out of her chair and moves to chat-mode. 'Now, there's plenty of food in the fridge. Wash up after yourself and I'll phone when I can to check you're OK. Don't go out. Be good. Yes?'

Nod (*repeat until door shuts*).

Go to next screen

I retreat to my room and switch on the computer. If only Real Life was as easy as a computer game. You know who the enemy is, hack off a few limbs, zap a few aliens, hijack a few cars and suddenly you're a hero.

But who is the enemy? Is it Tempus? Is it Nova? Or is it me? I spend a few hours hacking, zapping and hijacking but it doesn't make me feel any better. For the first time in my life computer games don't block out the real world.

I shut down, switch off and mooch around my room with nothing to do. Next thing I find myself dragging my old toybox out from under the bed and taking it downstairs.

Then I switch on the TV and watch all those children's cartoons I used to love when I was little. At the same time I start building a massive mega-town out of building blocks, watched by all the toys and teddies I've lined up on the floor. Retro-games or what?

Brrrinnnggg!

The doorbell disturbs my afternoon play. I check my watch and am surprised to see it's 4.00 p.m. already. It's cyberM's late night at the salon and she's not due back yet, so security checks are in order.

I stand behind the locked door.

'Who is it?'

'Me!' (Girl's voice. I suspect it's Anna.)

'Who's me?'

'Anna.' (Name confirmed.)

'Sorry. Restricted access. Please enter the password.'

'Password? Oh, I don't know, er... *palindrome.*'

'Your password has not been accepted.'

'Oh, come on, Jamie. Please let me in. I need to see you.'

'There is no one here with that name. Would you like to re-enter the password?'

'Yes please, *cyberJ*!'

'Go ahead.'

'OK, er...hero.com!'

'Password confirmed. This is a serious security risk! How did you know that?'

'Just open up and I'll tell you!'

LEVEL 13
Reboot

I unlock the door and Anna blasts through on overdrive. 'Your screen-saver says *hero.com*,' she says. 'I saw it the other day, remember?'

'Oh, yeah. I knew that. Just testing,' I say coolly.

'Anyway, I came to tell you that we had our Clean-up Campaign meeting yesterday and it was so flat without you. You're the one with all the ideas, cyberJ. We need you!'

'That's what all the girls say!' I smile, suddenly catching sight of the TV room with my toys and teddies. 'Er, let's go in the kitchen, shall we?'

'We need your ideas for the publicity push on the Clean-up Campaign – we want posters and leaflets to really fire people up!'

Her eyes are bright like a flashing graphic.

'Anna, I'm not going to play games with you… I went to see Nova yesterday – to warn him about your plans—'

'You...you traitor, Jamie! Why?'

'Because I thought a sports centre was a good idea, but—'

'You can still have your sports centre! I've been talking to my dad about it. He said they'd just build it on a brown field that's all.'

'Yeah? Well, Poo Park is the brownest field I've ever seen. No contest.'

'No, you don't get it! A brown field is land that's already been used for something else – and it can be used again. Like that old bottle factory on the edge of town…'

Suddenly it clicks. *Double clicks.* 'We can have the sports centre *and* save the park! Cool. You know my dad used to train a kids' football team in that park. He said it was the heart and lungs of Grimly…'

Anna starts waving her nail-blades round in danger-mode. 'So, why'd you warn Nova? You two-faced, lying, cheating—'

'Hey, you're attacking the wrong person – Nova's the cheat,' I say, edging out of the way of her silver spears. 'He's destroyed some record that said the park was *common land.* Mean anything to you?'

'*Common land*? We did that in History...' she drums her nails on the kitchen table and I stand well back. 'Hmm, yeah...it's land that belongs to everyone so they can walk and play and feed their cows—'

'No! You mean we can't take our cows to Poo Park any more? That's criminal!'

'Well, if you're not going to take this seriously I'm leaving...'

She tries to push past me but I stand my ground, risking death by nail-blade. 'Don't go, Anna. I *am* serious. I can see how important the park is to Grimly – we've got to stop Nova.'

She looks me straight in the eye. 'Really? How do I know you're telling the truth this time, cyberJ?'

'You have the word of a hero.com,' I say. 'I'll do anything to stop him.'

'Hmm, OK then. How about hacking into his e-mail?'

'But I don't have his password! Anyway, what good will that do? Can't we just get

The Grim Times group together and launch an all-out missile attack on the Nova World building?'

'CyberJ, get real! If we access his e-mail we might find some proof of his dodgy deal. But if your computer skills aren't up to it, then—'

'Just start the clock and watch me hack.'

Anna follows me to my room, waits for me to switch on my computer and log into Nova's website. Then she starts the countdown.

'10–9'

First I locate the clue Nova's left to remind him of his password: **walktall**.

'8–7'

Easy. The password must be **thinkbig**. I type it in and wait…

'6–5'

Password rejected. Please try again.

'4–3'

Nooo! – it's got to be *think big*! Nova lives by those words and now he's too big. Ahh, that's it! I press **Caps Lock** and try again: **THINKBIG**.

'2—'

Password accepted.

'You've done it, cyberJ!' Nova's in-box list flashes on screen and there's one saved message on it.

'It's from the council,' Anna blasts in my ear. 'Open it. What's it say?'

I double click and we read:

From: D.Simms@grimlycouncil.gov
To: Nova@novaworld.com
Subject: Grimly Park

Dear Nova,

I want to thank you for the large sum of money you agreed to give towards a new sports centre today. In view of this, Grimly Council has brought forward the MAKE GRIMLY GREAT planning meeting. We will discuss future plans for Grimly Park on Tuesday 29th April at 5.00p.m. at Grimly Town Hall. We hope to see you there.

Best wishes,

Councillor Simms

Anna checks her watch. 'The meeting starts in half an hour. We have to do something!'

'What?'

'I don't know. We'll think of that when we get there. Come on, cyberJ!'

'But I…I'm grounded – and I'm trying to win back points with cyberM.'

'Your mum? What time does she finish work?'

'Seven o'clock. It's her late night.'

'We'll be back before then – and she wants to save the park, too, doesn't she?'

I can't argue with that. 'Yeah, but we'll have to run – we've missed the bus.'

'D'you know any short cuts?'

'If we go into town by the back streets we might just make it in time but it's a bit of a maze—'

'So what are we waiting for? Let's go!'

That's another rule from the **Sacred Cybercode** – *Never Turn Down a Challenge.*

LEVEL 14

Maze Race

Anna and I exit the house on full speed. We shoot up The Cut, take a left on Dark Lane and right on Maze Street.

Suddenly we hit a brick wall which seems to have sprung up out of nowhere!

'Now...what?' Anna's gulping for breath but she's not ready to give up yet.

'We can't climb over – I don't fancy the broken glass on top of that wall. We could cut through those gardens if you can manage those fences—'

Before I can finish, Anna throws herself at the fence in full-on female warrior mode and I scramble after her.

Halfway across the first garden something catches my eye. It's coming from a side window – a cloud of black smoke.

'Anna, stop!' I yell after her.

She doesn't turn but I hear her shout, 'Come on, Jamie. We've got to save the park!'

She's right but my legs won't move. What if there's someone in the house?

'You go on, Anna. Do what you can – I'll catch you up!'

There's no time to think. I run to the back of the house and hammer on the door. 'Hello? Hello? Anyone in there?'

Nothing.

I try the door handle and nearly fall into the hall. The smoke hasn't reached this far – there's just a bad smell of burning.

The door to the first room is half open. A quick scan shows me an old lady in a chair.

I move slowly towards her. Is she alive? I try to keep calm – if she is I don't want to give her a shock and scare her to death.

Her hand is warm when I take it, so I pat it a bit, whispering, 'Hello? Hel-lo…'

Then her eyes flicker open. 'It's OK, don't worry – you need to get out, that's all,' I say. 'There's smoke coming from your kitchen.'

'Oh dear, I put a pan of milk on and I thought I'd just sit down for a minute—'

'You'll be alright. Let's get you out of here. D'you need any help?'

She's struggling out of the chair and takes my arm for support. She's thin and trembling but as we shuffle to the door she suddenly stops. 'What about Flossie? She was in her basket, I'll have to get her—'

She turns to go back but I put an arm around her shoulder and guide her to the door saying, '*I'll* get her. Is she your cat, then?'

'Yes, oh I do hope she's alright.'

We come out of the door just as Anna's running up to it.

'Jamie, what—'

I put my fingers to my lips. 'Shh, it's OK. I'm just going to get this lady's cat, Anna. Can you wait with her for a minute?'

Anna takes her arm as I run back to the side door. Through the open window I can see a pan smouldering on the stove and a towel on fire.

I can see an empty basket, too, but no sign of

the cat so I slowly open the door, crouching down low to avoid any exploding glass and fire-balls.

Miaow!

There's a blood-curdling howl, everything goes black and I'm attacked by a spitting, clawing furball.

'*Gerroffme!*' I yell, tumbling backwards in a reverse-roll, wrestling with this demon before it rips me to death.

'Flossie!' I hear as the demon's claws are dug out of my chest.

I risk opening my eyes to see the old lady reaching out for the furry body. Anna's there too with some neighbours.

Someone helps me to my feet while hands are slapping me on the back. (Double pain-points.) They're going, 'Good lad', 'Well done', 'He's a bloomin' hero', but I don't know what all the fuss is about.

A man shakes my hand, saying, 'Don't worry, we called the fire brigade. Now, what's your name?'

At the same time Anna's tugging my arm, saying, 'We've got to go now, can you make it?'

'Sorry, can't stop – bye, Flossie, take care of your owner!' I wave and race off down the drive with Anna.

We hit the main street and a siren is shrieking towards us like an extra-loud special effect. *Nee-Nawww! Nee-Nawww! Nee-nawww!*

There's no time to stay and watch all the action – we're already flying in the opposite direction.

Go To Next Screen

It's ten to six. We've missed the start of the meeting but we might get there before it ends. We're racing up the Town Hall steps when an attendant blocks us.

'Now then, slow down. Where's the fire?'

'Planning...meeting...about the park,' Anna gulps out. 'We're reporting for the school newspaper.'

The man checks his sheet, checks his watch and checks his sheet again. He'd have no chance in a beat-the-clock game.

Then he speaks into his walkie talkie.

'Foxtrot Alpha, this is Tango Delta. Are you there? Over.'

'I'm here, Tango, Delta. Go ahead. Over.'

'Can you advise status of planning meeting? Over.'

'Meeting just over. Over.'

'Thank you, Foxtrot Alpha. Over and out.'

He switches it off and shakes his head. 'Sorry, the meeting's over.'

He's not exactly a master of surprise.

Just then we hear voices. A group of men and women appear on the stairs – at the centre of them is Nova. He's got a big smile on his face and when he sees us he breaks from the group and comes our way.

'CyberJ – good to see you!' he says, but his eyes are bouncing around like lasers from me to Anna and back again.

'So, you guys are friends now, yeah? Well, if you came for the meeting you're too late. The Nova Sports Centre is a done deal. We'll make a start by digging up the park—'

'That park is *common land* and it belongs to the people of Grimly, you cheat!' Anna's in

Queen of the Palindromes mode now and she stabs a nail-blade under Nova's nose.

He steps back smartly. 'I suggest we continue this chat in private before you lose total control,' he says and opens the door behind him.

We follow him in and I close the door, keeping my fingers on the handle ready for a quick exit.

'OK, what've you got? Shoot,' he fires at Anna.

'We know you cheated and when we tell everyone you'll lose the right to build on the park,' Anna hits back.

'Cheated? No idea what you're talking about. It's the word of two kids against me. Got any proof?'

We've got no ammo and he knows it. So I try an alternative strategy.

'If you move the sports centre to the old bottle factory site, Nova, you get your dream, we get our green – it's a win-win scene!' I say.

'Build on the bottle factory site? Yeah, OK.' He's smiling and I can't believe it. We win. If only all games were this easy!

Then he reloads. 'Sure I'll build there – office blocks and apartments – after I've built on the park. By the time I've finished they might as well rename Grimly and call it Nova Town.'

Then he's laughing his Power-Mad-Maniac laugh and my fingers are turning the door handle.

'You wait till next Sunday,' Anna fires a parting shot as we make our exit. 'The people of Grimly won't let the park go without a fight!'

'Next Sunday?' Nova pulls out a gadget and punches a few buttons. 'Thanks for the warning – I'll make some plans.'

LEVEL 15

Press Escape

'You'd make a good gamer, Anna,' I say as we walk down the Town Hall steps.

'Hmm, what makes you think that?'

'The way you handled Nova – you never give up, do you?'

Anna shrugs her shoulders. She slows down and suddenly all the fight seems to have gone out of her.

'I dunno, cyberJ. It's easy for you to talk – you're a real hero.'

'What?'

'The woman and the fire! Have you forgotten already?'

'Fire? Hmm, saving an old woman and her cat from a burning milk pan isn't exactly a high scorer on the hero scale.'

'Come on, get real! You were amazing – you acted so fast and you didn't think about yourself. I just stood there like I had brain fog.'

'Quick reflexes – classic game player features,' I say modestly. 'I practised on that game *Blazing Inferno Flame-Fest*!'

'And you worked out the password so we could hack into his mail – you're a hero.com too.'

We're at the bottom of her street now and it's getting dark. She stops in the pool of light under a lamppost and her glasses are mirrored in silver so I can't read her eyes.

'But unless we can think of something good to get people to the park on Sunday, we've lost and Nova knows it,' she says sadly.

'No, that's not how gamers talk, Anna. OK, so we've lost this battle but you don't give in. You take a break and play the level again. Try new tactics. We'll think of something tomorrow—'

'Thanks, cyberJ…'

And then she launches a surprise attack – a lip-on-lip direct hit! (Cherry and kiwi flavour if I'm not mistaken.) My defences are down so she ups the time factor, too. The attack lasts well over thirty seconds!

Now I'm the one with brain fog. If Anna's trying to zombify me then she's halfway there! I feel like my brain is melting and will dribble out of my ears at any minute.

It's Critical Romance-Overload Danger level. With a superhuman effort I regain control of myself and pull back.

'Gotta go, Anna. See you tomorrow!' I gulp.

Press: **Escape**

Press: **Run**

Go to next screen

Luckily I get home just before cyberM. If she knew I'd gone out when I was grounded she'd have a full-on freak-out-fest. I even have time to get a cup of tea ready to gain max points.

'Jamie – is that you?' she calls out as soon as she opens the door.

'Well, who else would it be? I'm in the kitchen.'

She comes in looking more of a zombie than ever. Her eyes are red in her pale face and her mascara's run a bit.

'Mum, are you OK? I've made you some tea.'

'Why didn't you answer the phone, Jamie? I called half an hour ago. You haven't been out, have you?'

'Er...no. I must have had my headphones on, sorry.'

She crumples into a chair. She's not really a zombie at all, I think. She's just a worried worn-out woman and it's all my fault.

'Are you hungry? Can I get you something? I do a very good beans on toast.'

She smiles. 'OK, thanks! And put the radio on, too. Let's have some music in this café.'

I switch it on but it's seven o'clock so we get the news first. I'm not really listening until I hear:

'And finally on Grimly news – a young hero rescued eighty-four-year-old Margaret Green from the flames today when a fire broke out in her home on Maze Street.

Firefighter Steve Lang was on the scene and this is what he said, "Mrs Green was asleep when the youngster spotted the fire in the kitchen. He led her to safety before she was overcome by fumes. He even went back for Mrs Green's cat, Flossie, who means the world to her!

"We put out the flames and Mrs Green wanted to thank her young rescuer. But the shy hero and his friend ran off without giving their names—"'

'Maze Street? That's not very far away, is it?' cyberM says.

'Dunno.' Luckily I have my back to her so she can't see my face.

'Well, it's nice to hear some good news for a change, isn't it?' cyberM goes on.

'Can't see what all the fuss is about myself,' I say. 'Now, does Madam want ketchup with her meal?'

After tea I wash the dishes (at least ten more points) before going to my room. My fingers are itching to hack into Nova's account again and see if I can find some vital piece of data to help us.

As soon as I go on-line a message comes up:

```
Message from annaT to cyberJ

annaT:    Hi, it's Anna.
          Wanna chat?

cyberJ:   Not right now, gimme
          5 mins.

annaT:    Ok c u l8ter.
```

After five minutes I'm ready to chat.

```
Message from cyberJ to annaT

cyberJ:   Hey, Anna. Nova's
          making plans.

annaT:    Waddya mean?

cyberJ:   Tell u 2morrow. I've
          found something out.
```

annaT: C'mon gimme a clue or
          I won't sleep tonite.

cyberJ: can't risk it U never
          know who might be
          hacking thro cyberspace
     rite now.

annaT: Grrrrrrrrrr!

cyberJ: c u at break 2morrow in
     3D land.

annaT: I'm counting the hours.
     xx

I stare at the screen. X marks the spot.

Is Anna cyberflirting? Am I supposed to X back? I am getting to like Anna but she's so full-on, it's scary. I'm not ready for an X life – I need a training session!

Once again I take the Game Player's way out and press: **Escape**.

LEVEL 16

Stop-the-Tot

'Tots.'

'Pardon?'

I've only just met up with Anna in the Resource Centre and already she's talking in code.

'Tots,' she repeats. 'You know, one level up from rug-rats. Toddlers, little kids.'

'Huh?'

'Mrs Li says we can go to Grimly Nursery this afternoon to tell them about the park and the Clean-up Campaign. Tomorrow we visit the Junior School. When the kids go home and tell their mums and dads about it we'll get whole families along on Sunday.'

'Yeah? Well, newsflash! Nova's going, too. I found out last night. He's going to bring this massive model of "Grimly in the Future" to the park. He thinks that'll win people over.'

'So it's war, then,' Anna says. She puts on

her scary Queen of the Palindromes face. 'Well, we'll show him. What's your new strategy for the Clean-up Campaign? I can't wait to hear it.'

'Er, well...' My mind is as blank as a blank screen but luckily Anna interrupts me.

'What they need is a hero,' she says. 'Someone they can believe in. Someone to get them fired up—'

'Yeah, right. Captain Clean-up to the rescue!' I say.

'That's it! You've done it again, cyberJ! I knew you'd save the day. You could dress up and—'

'Press stop, right now, Anna. I was joking – superheroes are so retro! My type of hero does not wear tight lycra and a fancy cape.'

'OK,' Anna stops on thinking mode. Then she reboots. 'You could go more…er *cyber-chic*. Like…well, what you're wearing now. Long black coat, boots, shades and maybe a green T-shirt to represent the green park—'

'And what about you, then?' I fire her ammo right back at her.

'Me?'

'Yeah, what's Penny Playpark going to wear?'

'No, I—'

'The girls need a hero, too,' I say, hammering home the attack.

She sighs. 'Penny Playpark's wearing black and green, too, I suppose.'

Yes! I win. Double-max points!

...Or is it? Now it hits me full on. I've just said yes to standing up to a class full of tots posing as Captain Clean-up. How sad is that?

And another thing. TOT. That's a palindrome, isn't it? Is this one of Anna's traps? Are we really equal partners in a fight for what's right or is this just part of her plan to steal my cyber-soul (and body)?

Advance to next screen

'Fingers on your lips, children. We have two very important visitors today, so—'

'Is it Father Christmas?'

'Is it Rudolph?'

'No, Tanya, no, Nathan. Not in April. It's Captain Clean-up and Penny Playpark!'

We open the door and nothing can prepare us for the full horror of these ferocious ankle-biters.

Level 16:	**Stop-the-Tot**
Location:	**Cyber-nursery**
Task:	**Mega-mouthed ankle-biters eat anything, including *you*. Stop them!**

Scroll down Weapons Menu

Select> Concrete cookie

Difficulty rating: Easy

Aim a cookie at tot to stop it.

Tots: *Dribble! Drool! Toddle!*

Fire 1! Fire 2! Fire 3!

You win!

Next screen

Difficulty rating: Impossible

Tots: *Dribble! Drool! Toddle! Sing!* – a lethal combo!

Fire1! Fire2!...

You lose!

Dribble! Drool! Toddle! Sing!

'The wheels on the bus go round and round...'

Anna and I are standing back-to-back in a crowd of singing tots who are crushing our kneecaps...

'Children, be quiet! It's not rhyme time yet!' The teacher comes rushing to our rescue.

They switch from music-mode to chat-mode.

'Look at my new tooth!'

'I've got red knickers.'

'Dribble, drool, hic!'

But the teacher is well-armed with secret weapons. 'Now, sit on your bottoms please and move back.'

I'll say this for her, the *bum-shuffle* works instantly. Then she adds the *fingers-on-your-lips* move – a powerful combo!

'Very good,' she pauses, scanning the scene of seated tots with expert eyes. 'Adam, I said "lips", dear. "Fingers on lips." Not there. No, not on Ravi's lips. *There.* That's it. Good.'

'OK, so it's over to Captain Clean-up and Penny Playpark to tell you why they're here...'

Go to end of Level

Time to move on. I'm not going to replay the tot-tastic dribble-fest for you screen-by-screen in all its slimy horror.

Let's just say it's one of the hardest levels I've ever played. We had to use all our weapons, including singing, smiling and shoelace tying but in the end it worked.

It turns out that the littl'uns are the most lethal. After that the older classes we saw the next day were a pushover. Everyone wants to dress up as Captain Clean-up or Penny Playpark and come to the clean-up on Sunday.

Oh and I threw in an extra bonus feature. A treasure hunt. Anna calls it a cheat, but if Nova can do it, so can I.

It involves money.

Lots of it.

Chocolate money.

LEVEL 17

The Final Showdown?

Select Day:	**Sunday 30th April**
Select Weather:	**Sunshine**
Select People:	**How many?**
Captain Clean-up:	**1**
Penny Playpark:	**1**
***The Grim Times* Group:**	**6**
Clean-up Campaign Supporters:	**??**

Anna and cyberJ (aka you-know-who) walk to Grimly Park in the morning sunshine. We're blown away by the army of supporters on the streets.

'That publicity blitz really hit home,' Anna says proudly as we pass yet another poster with a photo of us and the words:

Be a hero – clean-up Grim Park!
Show the Council, keep it green!

Everywhere we look there are whole families of Captain C. and Penny P. clones. They come in small, medium and large sizes, all dressed in black and green, with cool shades.

The Grim Times group members hand out weapons for the battle as we enter the park – hedge-cutters, litter-pickers and plastic bags. Some teachers are helping them, and I am surprised to see Mrs Li, Tempus and CyberM dressed in black and green outfits, too – way out of character!

Press: **Start**

Everyone sets to like warriors – hacking bushes, slashing weeds and terminating litter and dog poo.

At lunchtime we get together in the main field at the front of the park for a well-earned picnic. All the families have brought different types of food from sandwiches and samosas to cream-cakes and black-eyed peas.

We're just about to launch a full-on food-fest when a black shiny car pulls up at the gates.

Out step the mayor and mayoress, looking a bit overdressed for a picnic in their robes and gold chains. Then a few more cars follow and download some men and women from Grimly Council.

Finally a mega-removal-van parks up and Nova gets out. He starts giving orders to a team of men in white overalls who off-load a huge plastic model of 'Grimly-in-the-Future'. It's so big it takes ten men to carry it into the park.

The mayor stands near it and speaks. 'People of Grimly, I'm glad to see so many of you here today helping clear up Grim Park. It's been an eyesore for years and—'

'*Booo!* ' Some of the families let the mayor know what they think of him knocking their park.

He holds up his hands as if to surrender.

'Yes, I know some of you want to keep the park and clean it up but with Nova's help we can upgrade our town completely. I'm sure you'll agree when you see the sports centre in the middle here.' He points to a big grey block with NOVA printed on it. 'So, together we can MAKE GRIMLY GREAT! Now, any questions?'

Anna puts her hand up.

'Yes, the young lady there.'

'Excuse me, Mr Mayor, but did you ask the people of Grimly if they might want to *move* the sports centre so we can *keep* the park?'

'I, er...' the mayor turns and whispers to Nova.

Anna doesn't wait. 'Well, we think it must stay. A park means fun, games and freedom!'

That's my signal. 'TREASURE HUNT!' I yell at the top of my voice, opening sacks and throwing gold coins into the air.

Now it's raining chocolate money on Nova's model city.

'*Yeeaaahhhh!!!!*' the tots scream as they scramble forward and the fun begins...

'Stop them!' yells Nova as tots – all dressed up as Captain C. and Penny P. clones – pile into his Nova-town. '...but don't hurt them!' he adds as some of the parents start booing.

'Come 'ere!' Nova's army of heavies are on the scene in seconds, but they're no match for hyper-tots on a chocolate hunt.

Crawl! Climb! Wriggle! Giggle!

The tots climb up, down and over the model, ignoring the grabbing hands reaching out for them.

Aaahhhh! they sigh, sitting down to unwrap the coins and ramming them in their mouths. *Mmmm! Slobber! Dribble, Drool!*

Awww! the crowd goes, enjoying the cute and innocent scene of total greed.

The heavies shrug their shoulders – they know when they're beaten.

Now the model town is littered like a battle-ground with finger marks and stains showing where the action took place.

Everyone in the park is laughing and cheering. Even the mayor is smiling as some reporters rush forward to snap a few photos.

'I'm glad to see our new town is so popular with the young folk of Grimly,' he says.

'Is that the final showdown? Did we win or lose, cyberJ?' Anna whispers in my ear.

I shake my head. 'The Game's not over till it's over, Anna. I've just seen Nova leading his troop of heavies back to the removal van outside the park. He's up to something.'

She looks where I'm pointing just as Nova steps out of the van. He's carrying the ultimate weapon – a garden fork!

'Nova's going to dig up the park!' I yell. 'Call *The Grim Times* group *now*, Anna. *Red alert* – this is an emergency!'

LEVEL 18

Fighting Food-Fest

Our emergency meeting takes place at the back of the picnic tables.

'OK, troops. Nova's got a weapon-upgrade. We need to fight back fast! So what've we got?' I look round at our task force but they stare back blankly.

Out of the corner of my eye I can see Nova and his men marching back into the park, holding their garden forks over their shoulders like rifles.

'Nova's evil!' Anna fires off, suddenly. 'Let's poke out his eyes with a litter-picker and chop off his head with a hedge-cutter!' Her nail-blades flash dangerously as she mimes the moves.

'*Yeahh,*' the others mutter.

'OK, Anna, I like your style but we have to get real here,' I say. My voice is deep now and I sound like a grown-up – what's happening?

'We want Nova to lose face – not lose his life.'

'*Awww*,' the troops sound disappointed. That's not right. A hero.com has to keep their spirits up.

'We need a secret weapon,' I say, grabbing a sausage roll and loading up a ketchup bottle.

Spluurge!

I squeeze a bit too hard and a mega-dollop of red splashes over everything. Suddenly a whole **Weapons Menu** drops down right in front of my eyes.

'Food fight!' I whisper.

'Food fight – yes!' everyone fires back.

Time to act fast. 'OK, Imran, Grace and Gloria – you lead the tots and junior force. We're talking max splat-a-bility here. What have you got?'

'Yoghurt?'

'Check.'

'Squirty cream?'

'Check.'

'Sausages?'

'No, they bounce. That's for the next round—'

'Jelly?'

'Check…OK – move it! Next Laura, Josh and

Andy – we're upping the difficulty level here. You lead the older kids. We're talking missiles and torpedoes—'

'Spinning pizzas?'

'Check.'

'Slamming samosas?'

'Check.'

'Heat-seeking sausages?'

'Check...OK. Go, go, go!'

That leaves Anna and me. I put a squeezy ketchup bottle in her hand and salute. 'Now you're armed and extremely dangerous,' I say. 'Good luck, soldier.'

She salutes me back. 'Thanks, Captain Clean-up.'

I wink. 'Aka cyberJ.'

Then we hear Nova launch his final attack.

'OK, you've had your fun,' he says to the crowd, 'but we're here for a reason. Today we start digging and tomorrow the bulldozers move in!'

'*Booo!*'

His hard-faced men are lined up next to him with their heavy-metal weapons. They look straight ahead like robots and don't see the

Captain Clean-up and Penny Playpark clones crowding round the picnic tables.

Nova holds up his garden fork and everything goes quiet. It's our black and green army against his white-coated heavies. Each side stands to attention, waiting for a signal.

'People of Grimly, Lord Mayor – I have the honour of digging up the first piece of park!' Nova shouts, spearing the ground with his fork.

At that moment Anna and I squeeze our ketchup bottles, letting rip with both barrels—

Splurge!

Perfect timing! A giant red splash arcs up high in the sky and comes down *Splat!* smack in the middle of Nova's face. Yes! A direct hit!

'Start digging!' Nova splutters through dripping ketchup.

'*Food fight!!*' I yell. 'Fire 1!'

Splam! Splat!

A trail of strawberry yoghurt streaks through the air and lands on one of the heavies' head, followed by the yoghurt pot itself.

'Fire 2!'

Skkkwooooooshhh! Squirty cream blasts

straight at the heavies wreaking havoc.

'Fire 3!'

Blaammm! Blob! Blob! Blob!

A jelly and ice-cream bomb blitz rains down – shame to waste good food, but this is a life or death situation.

'Reload!'

The heavies are dripping in raspberry ripple, chocolate sauce, jelly and squirty cream. Some of them drop their spades and walk off – I don't think Nova pays them enough for this type of aggro. Others stand their ground and start digging – Nova included.

'Time for the big guns! Three hits and they're out!'

Ready, take aim...Fire!

Swizzzz! Swizzzz! Swizzzzz!

Sausages, samosas and pizzas fly through the air, and everyone in the whole park cheers.

'*STOP!*' The mayor is wiping his face with a handkerchief and looking nervous. 'Stop this terrible chaos and carnage!' (Bit of an exaggeration, but a great name for a computer game.)

'For the sake of peace and the people of Grimly, I am going to cancel the plans to build on the park. We'll find out what everyone wants first and—'

'*Raaaaaay!!!*' The rest of his words are lost in a victory cry from the crowd.

'Game over, you win, cyberJ!' Anna whispers in my ear.

Yes – victory! Now I'm the ultimate hero.com. Master of the—

Just then someone grabs my arm and croaks in my ear, 'You're the one, aren't you, dear?'

People pause and look round – including *The Grim Times* group, cyberM, Tempus and Mrs Li.

'It's you, isn't it? Ooh you're special, aren't you? My mystery hero.'

I look at the little old lady blankly.

'You're the one who saved my Flossie!' she says, launching a surprise lip-on-lip attack.

It's a direct hit – lavender and mothball flavoured! These female warriors are all the same, ancient or modern. Don't they know any other moves?

Awww! Now everyone's smiling and clapping and saying, 'Look at Jamie. Isn't that sweet?'

OK, so if this is Real Life, I've just got one question.

Where's the **Escape** key when you need it?

LEVEL 19

Select a Hero

THE GRIM TIMES – HERO EDITION

VICTORY FOR LOCAL HEROES

by Anna Tempus

The Grim Times group voted the people of Grimly as their heroes for turning out to save Grimly Park last week.

A new 'Friends of the Park' group will work with the mayor to improve it for everyone.

FOOD-FIGHT!

James Bradshaw (aka Captain Clean-up, aka cyberJ) was the leader of the winning food-fight force but he refused to take all the glory. 'Everyone played their part,' he said, 'and Anna Tempus was the controller behind the Clean-up Campaign.'

NOVA *EVOLVES*

In a surprise move Nova has agreed to help build an adventure playground for the park (see competition below). The mayor said that he has spoken to Nova about new plans for a sports centre, too. 'He has agreed to network with local people to find the best place for it. It's good for his business and good for Grimly,' he said.

NEWSFLASH!

DESIGN YOUR OWN ADVENTURE PLAYGROUND!

ENTER GRIMLY'S COMPETITION. IF YOU WIN, SEE YOUR DREAM COME TRUE!

(SEND YOUR ENTRY TO NOVA WORLD DESIGNS)

Who's your hero? Here's what some people in Grimly said:

Captain Clean-up. He gives us chocolate and he's got cool sunglasses.
Nathan Brown (5 yrs)

Penny Playpark. She's fun and she can tie shoelaces.
Ravi Usman (4 yrs)

CyberJ aka Jamie Bradshaw – he's a hero.com. He's got the best ideas, the best computer skills and he helped keep Grimly Green!
Anna Tempus (12 yrs)

Those two-legs Jamie and Anna. They saved me and my owner. Now she's joined The Friends of Grimly Park – Miaow!
Flossie (7 yrs)

My heroes are:
1. My mum – for putting up with me.

2. My dad – I found out some things about him I never knew.
3. Anna Tempus – a female warrior who never gives up.
CyberJ (nearly 13 yrs)

A hero is someone who keeps going day in and day out, learning when they lose as well as when they win. Everyone can be a hero!
Mrs Li (42 yrs)

Go to Bonus Level

'What d'you think?' Anna prints off the final draft of *The Grim Times* for me and I scan the front page.

'It's the dog's dangles,' I say.

'Well, that's one way of putting it,' she smiles. We're alone in the Resource Centre and I can predict her next move by now.

'Well, that's the end, then. Thanks for all your help. You've done your detention hours and Mrs Li says you're free to go.'

'OK,' I pause. Now for the lip-on-lip direct hit

but this time it will be different. This time I'm ready for it.

'Well, see you around, Ja…er, cyberJ?'

She waves her nail-blades and they flash in a friendly way, but that's all. What kind of a move is *that*? Is she set on a delayed timer or something?

I pause and wait a bit but nothing happens. 'Yeah, er, see you around Anna…'

I give her one last chance but she stands there as still as a frozen screen.

'Bye then.' I exit.

Exit Bonus Level

So maybe in real life the hero.com doesn't end up with the cyberbabe, I think as I get home. Somehow it takes the edge off winning the Game.

And in real life some of your best known figures can act way out of character. Like cyberM, for example.

When I get in she's lying down in a dark room, wearing a green eye-mask, listening to strange noises which sound like the sound FX in that game *Shrieking Alien Showdown*.

'What's going on? What's that noise?' I say, walking in on the scene.

She sits up and takes off her eye-mask. 'Ugh, is it that time already? I was just relaxing with my whale song tape on, that's all.'

'And what's that smell?'

'It must be the ylang-ylang candles. Very good for stress.'

'Are you OK?'

'Yes, I am now. Just needed some thinking therapy and it worked. I've made up my mind.'

'About what?'

'About Frank…er Mr Tempus. I know you don't like him and you were acting so strangely that I was really worried about you. But after you helped save the park and that old lady, I can see that you're still the same Jamie underneath. I don't want us to fight any more so I'm going to stop seeing him.'

'Oh…'

'You know, at one point I even blamed those computer games for your strange behaviour!

I didn't want to face up to what was really wrong. Sorry, Jamie. As if you aren't old enough to know the difference between a computer game and real life!'

'Ha!' I laugh loudly. A bit too loud – as if I can't control the volume.

'Anyway, it was getting difficult because Anna …well, she's got a bit of a crush on you so—'

'You think so? But she just blanked me when we said goodbye today. And now I've quit *The Grim Times* group we won't see much of each other any more.'

I didn't really mean to give cyberM so much data but the message popped up out of nowhere.

'Maybe she was waiting for you to give a signal that you liked *her*,' cyberM says. 'You do, don't you?'

'Sorry, that type of info is not for public access. It's like me asking if you like Mr Temp …er Frank.'

CyberM doesn't respond. She doesn't have to.

I sigh, 'You know. I don't *really* mind if you keep on seeing him, cyber...er Mum. It's *your* life.'

She stands up, pulls the curtains open and starts blowing out the candles. 'Thanks, Jamie. Now I know you're growing up, and I'll think about what you said—'

'As long as he doesn't move in overnight or anything. And as long as you don't meet him outside the school gates...that's way off limits.'

'I get the message! Working on *The Grim Times* has really improved your communication skills, Jamie. Maybe you should carry on with it.'

Go to Final Screen

After tea I log on-line and my fingers itch to chat with Anna. If I tell her I'm staying in *The Grim Times* group, will that be the signal she's looking for?

I wanted to be a hero in the Game but it didn't exactly play out how I expected. Leading a troop of anklebiters in a food-fight is not exactly the final showdown I had in mind. Still, Anna seemed quite impressed and if she needs more proof I can always flash my cat-claw scars at her.

And there are other versions of the Game just waiting to be played. I don't know if I'm quite ready for the full-on Dating Game yet, but a little bit of training can do no harm…

I log on to chat.

```
Message from cyberJ to annaT

cyberJ:   Hey Anna, when's the
          next Grim Times meeting?
          Let me know if you need
          some back-up and I'll
          be there...
```

Orchard Red Apples

Utterly Me, Clarice Bean	Lauren Child	1 84362 304 8
Clarice Bean Spells Trouble	Lauren Child	1 84362 858 9
The Fire Within	Chris d'Lacey	1 84121 533 3
IceFire	Chris d'Lacey	1 84362 373 0
The Poltergoose	Michael Lawrence	1 86039 836 7
The Killer Underpants	Michael Lawrence	1 84121 713 1
The Toilet of Doom	Michael Lawrence	1 84121 752 2
Maggot Pie	Michael Lawrence	1 84121 756 5
The Snottle	Michael Lawrence	1 84362 344 7
Nudie Dudie	Michael Lawrence	1 84362 647 0
What Howls at the Moon in Frilly Knickers?	Emily Smith	1 84121 808 1
When Mum Threw Out the Telly	Emily Smith	1 84121 810 3
The Secret Life of Jamie B, SuperSpy	Ceri Worman	1 84362 389 7
The Secret Life of Jamie B, Rapstar	Ceri Worman	1 84362 390 0

All priced at £4.99

Orchard Red Apples are available from all good bookshops, or can be ordered direct from the publisher: Orchard Books, PO BOX 29, Douglas IM99 1BQ
Credit card orders please telephone 01624 836000
or fax 01624 837033 or visit our Internet site: www.wattspub.co.uk
or e-mail: bookshop@enterprise.net for details.

To order please quote title, author and ISBN
and your full name and address.
Cheques and postal orders should be made payable to 'Bookpost plc.'
Postage and packing is FREE within the UK
(overseas customers should add £1.00 per book).

Prices and availability are subject to change.